BOA
EDITIONS
LIMITED

METEOROLOGY

* * *

Poems by

Alpay Ulku

Foreword by

Yusef Komunyakaa

BOA EDITIONS, LTD. ✳ ROCHESTER, NY ✳ 1999

LC #: 97-74815
ISBN: 978-1-880238-72-1 paperback

First Edition
99 00 01 7 6 5 4 3 2 1

Publications by BOA Editions, Ltd. –
a not-for-profit corporation under section 501 (c) (3)
of the United States Internal Revenue Code –
are made possible with the assistance of grants from
the Literature Program of the New York State Council on the Arts,
the Literature Program of the National Endowment for the Arts,
the Lannan Foundation, the Sonia Raiziss Giop Charitable Foundation,
the Eric Mathieu King Fund of The Academy of American Poets,
as well as from the Mary S. Mulligan Charitable Trust,
the County of Monroe, NY, and from many individual supporters
including Richard Garth & Mimi Hwang, Judy & Dane Gordon,
Robert & Willy Hursh, and Pat & Michael Wilder.

Cover Design: Daphne Poulin-Stofer
Typesetting: Scribe Typography
Manufacturing: McNaughton & Gunn, Lithographers
BOA Logo: Mirko

BOA Editions, Ltd.
Richard Garth, Chair
A. Poulin, Jr., President & Founder (1976–1996)
260 East Avenue
Rochester, NY 14604

for my Anne-Marie

Contents

Foreword

Alpay Ulku's first book, *Meteorology*, has been conceived at the nucleus of a beautiful and painful sense of history. He has a mature sensibility which helps to conjure an engaging poetry that strikes the armor of the modern heart; his is an assured sense of aesthetics, but these poems would not feel as half as urgent and truthful if we didn't realize such treasured moments of distilled imagination and imagistic thrust were not raised from the knowledge of history. This poetry has not been prettied up to be attractive: its agency has been earned through a taut precision in language.

A cluster of short sentences and fragments is at the beginning of this wonderful book – as if the paper and ink are learning to breathe – that signals the internal architecture of this collection. In many ways, *Meteorology* shows how small things and commonplace elements collide to create a lively narrative. Moments add up to a significant vision. It shows the evolution of tension and mystery: conflict in the quietest place and serenity in the eye of the storm. This poetry reveals a tableau of contradictions at the center of our existence, showing what it means to be human. The entry to this collection is "July," in full heart of a revealing, cinematic moment: "The Emperor's moon is an orange smudge. His sky, his heat wave. His dust / is everywhere, on the leaves, over the arc lamps. On the doorsteps people sit on drinking beer. / They watch a jogger who doesn't belong there…" In this short excerpted passage, we are already at the center of the drama. It unfolds. It mystifies. "The Emperor's moon" rushes us to an unspoken historical terror – something that has been said without saying it; insinuated through silence.

Ulku is a master of juxtaposition. He plants little imagistic depth charges along the way. He seems to be aware of how one phrase lives beside another, how this dualism changes the whole picture – like musical notes. The silence. The said. The Space. The pace. And, in this sense, he knows that the brain will leap forth to create a connection. Ulku orchestrates and controls the tension in each poem. Here's a young poet who knows what to leave out, what to sacrifice without making his poetry oblique.

It seems that the weather is changing around the world. We hear "greenhouse effect" and "El Niño," but *Meteorology* is not about weather maps and climatic forecasts. If there's a weather in the heart and psyche, a millennial mist at the edge of our collective soul, Ulku's poems are more than digital exactitude and old-fashioned guesswork. The joy of inquiry weaves this book together. We are not told what to think, but we are made to feel that thinking is a human industry that separates us from the rest of the animal kingdom, that it is our gift and blessing. This poetry is fused from a quality of seeing that leads to insight, and the book could be seen as a small temple of images that won't let us escape scot-free. This collection holds us there, facing ourselves.

And when we close the book – this little door facing the storehouse of haunting images travels along in our heads. The last few lines propel us back up through the book's emotional symmetry, connecting us to that great symbol of American freedom (the car) cruising past in "West": "A car drives by, headlights on: the crunch of wheels on gravel / and the heater's low warm din lull the children asleep in the back seat. / A coyote crosses over to the other side, his eyes bright with hunger…" The car (horsepower). An open frontier still in the national psyche. Paradise. Possible happiness. Something to be conquered – even if it is ourselves, or our immense gluttonous imagination. Here, in the nomenclature of Ulku's weather, in this exhilarating cloud chamber of ideas and images, everything in the food of the gods.

– *Yusef Komunyakaa*

I

July

The Emperor's moon is an orange smudge. His sky, his heat wave.
        His dust
is everywhere, on the leaves, over the arc lamps. On the doorsteps people
        sit on drinking beer.
They watch a jogger who doesn't belong there. The light turns green, and
        a car just sits and idles.
Someone's looking to get shot, they mutter. A car horn blasts. His dams
        make the river run
backward, make it rise and make it fall. He makes it change its composition,
        makes it pure again.
Runoff and spillage. Fluoride, bleach. Islands of coal pushed by tugboats.
He makes glass and iron, and he takes our cancers away.
He digs lakes and lays fields to sustain us. The sweat down our backs
        dries deliciously
in the cool rooms where file servers keep accounts. He provides us
        with power.
Days that turn like a miller's wheel, nights the air in our lungs. His ashes
are everywhere, in the chambers where gasoline is trapped, compressed,
        and then ignited –
that's the force that drives the rods that make the engines work, in the tips
        of our cigarettes
flicked in the gutters. A car horn blasts. A window goes down. Someone
        yells something
about sleep. Shut up, someone replies. You go to hell. Why don't you
        come here and make me.

Bad Thoughts, Mixed Messages

It was after the nation-states broke down, and enclaves of races fought for
    power over continental trading blocks.

Normal people shot each other in the streets, just like that, though every
    living being is a cluster of data, unique, irreplaceable, the same
    as any other.

People spoke in capital letters as in the beginning of the gods or the one
    god, though every vision of the world is as good as any other.

Others raised their children in the high Mojave, without tools, while
    satellites raced from west to east: they have no one to teach them
    where to dig water in a dry wash, or what to do if the red cactus
    pricks them.

Or is it we who will die off, from the loneliness of believing nothing?

Or is this the start of a new age, underneath the yellow streetlights,
    the insects burning, drifting down through the stunned,
    sleepless trees?

After Completion

Only small things were possible in the centuries After Completion. Time
        was, a hundred thousand people could perish in battle over
        a hilltop. They died in terror, dreaming of home.
The north wind blows almost gently now, snapping the tips of the nettle
        trees, which multiply, and bear no fruit. Men and women hardly
        know each other. No one stumbles out of alleys with their
        clothes torn and smeared with blood.
Once, the black ants grew bolder, swarming the thresholds, the wheat
        and the corn, immune to poisons that would kill us. We made
        a paste of them, and they were good to eat.
You don't have to waste your life twisting the fear of death into different
        shapes.
When I finally came of age, I, too, made my god: a mix of Christ and
        Buddha, Black Elk, Gandhi, and Muhammad. It was a beautiful
        rite, with candles, and my closest friends and lovers.
In the heaven of our making, physics has two laws: shadows don't die,
        and shadows don't cast shadows.

Coin of the Realm

A twelve-year-old drags his rifle down the street like a toy wagon,
and his brothers raise their arms and celebrate with fire, calling
        freedom down:

flies are also plentiful. Everything else is black market. Rules which are or
        are not negotiable at any time.
Dust is also free. A palace guard drinks from his canteen. It's in him.
        The border

where interests intersect, switch sides. It's the ruins of a baby milk factory
        —no, poison gas.
The Second Spring of the 1960s, protest in the air. And then we up and
        won. CNN and CIA.

Days that change like the frames of a videotape. Days like a mouse in
        a maze.
Others watch the watchers, their choice in colas, credit cards, run their
        names and numbers.

Civilization is a fly growing eyes on its legs, its body. Switch it on and
        switch it off.
A big galoot, harmless and put-upon, nodding yup, yup.

Heat Lightning, Progress, Cat, George Orwell

It is a cat walking on rice paper.
It is a priest placing communion wafers on the penitents' clean red
       tongues.
Something is trying to wake up from a nightmare,
tapping the screen with its white wing – both wings.
It is the Morse code of an old-fashioned telegraph,
the kind that killed the Wild West. It is the eye of the pyramid.
Ezra Pound said: What *is* money?
A blind man's cane to follow the cat's paws.
The gathering storm is possible because the sky is cooling off.
If the storm can't be stopped, could the cooling?
Someone flings a window open. Takes a breath.

Ars Poetica

Then this happens, so that happens. And you're older again.
The sky, a cast-iron door, shuts without your consent:
some sickly stars. Déjà vu
is what happens when you know you could stop.
All this thinking, and you're still there.
Not even the right questions. So you put it down
to the long commute home. Open a beer.
It's hard enough just making friends.
Just making the time to eat right and shower.
To visit the zoo, see the cheetahs,
and still speak the enemy's language.
Use dignity, and another word for what it takes to survive.
The way they pace around. As if someone, some intimation tells them to
make this smaller place their own. Tells them, yes. Tells them a lie.

Spring Forward, Fall Back

Be a facilitator, not a roadblock, says the lady who runs the news stand,
    when the children reach for the comics,

BROTHER, CAN YOU SPARE A DIME? playing as she dances sixty years
    ago, her hair falling over her soldier's arm,

the scent of peaches. Are you my son? she whispers. The *Times,* please,
    smiles the man. Are a changin', she always replies.

And after three days of unpaid "training," the new telemarketers are
    replaced with more of where they came from.

Even his secretary, fresh from college, knows to clock herself out and
    stay, though the light falls at 5 P.M., falls and falls.

Hard times are hand-me-downs tossed to the youngest and the poorest.
    The 1960s were a crock of shit.

Tune in, turn on, drop out, smiles the son. Clean, don't lean, the lady
    replies, hands him the *Times* and his change back,

the first snow wheeling over the city, how if you look just right, you could
    believe we were moving.

Intermittent

You put out the moon your candle.
In the darkness the highway's a curl of smoke.

Only the sleepers afloat in their bodies
remember the way to the home world,

and they are not the ones so enthralled by others' strong convictions.
The holy man who keeps shouting through a bullhorn

Tonight is the end of the world
for fifteen years has frightened even the secret police.

Go to sleep. There may yet come a sign
for those who don't read meanings where there are none.

If you should set the roses on fire, the fish and the seas.
If you should let the grain keep rotting in the fields, bought and paid for.
Is it relief that sways the leaves at midnight or regret?
Or is it just the wind, a warm air mass, pressure, certain laws.

A dragonfly lights on a sprinkler head.

Off-Planet News

You're the place mentioned in all the brochures. ADVENTURE THE
SUNBELT
captioned beneath, the letters drawn with subliminal sexual poses mixed
inside.

In them, you're promising peace at last, and you succeed.
You turn the wheels that run the story

where memory is fluent with its constant self-eradication –
and that is the only constant.

You're a planet in its biosphere phase.
The proverbial snake devouring its own tail. Not a zero but a binary
code, an eye

opening. Where matter enters, becomes data,
and solitude is transferred from one place to another, while entropy waits
in vain.

You're a coin sent spinning on its edge.
Dying is a word we use for the thrill of it.

The Little Green Men of Summer

come a hundred to a package, but according to the Myers-Briggs, there
	are sixteen types.
One clutches binoculars as if they could save him, sees a thing, then sees
	it closer.
Two have the world in their gunsights, poised and loyal; when their
	day comes
they'll seize it: one with a sniper's lightning snap and the other,
	entrenched
in his nest with a mounted gun, by carving an opening his men can
	spring through.
The walking man is out of step, his rifle slung carelessly over his
	shoulder, thinking
of that line about the summer grasses — he's not well-liked, a dreamer
	and a dime a dozen.
The one with the handgun is cruel, quick, and easily provoked, a black
	marketeer, maybe.
The crawling man, he's a survivor; the bazooka guy shoulders the weight
	of the world;
one lobs grenades; some shoot from the hip; the mine sweepers come one
	to a package;
and the little god is free, an unadvertised special, scattering the men like
	exotic seeds
in the tailpipes of cars, over the train tracks, playing flood with a garden
	hose,
invasion of the giant ants, playing earthquake and firestorm, search
	and destroy.

History

Even this far from that burning place
the dogs would not stop howling.

When we gathered by the river
our captors told us our captors had been destroyed.

O City of Pure Light,
they razed what they had rebuilt in your name.

When the tinsmith's son stole from the grocer's cart,
we cut off his right hand, and fed it to the dogs.

I'm not saying it was wrong.
I knew the tinsmith, learned a song from the grocer.

But what we did to the woman who read the future in our coffee grounds
and spoke of what she saw.

I'm not saying what: I am no fool:
I did not want to die:

I took my harp down from the willow tree
and sang.

When they flung their copper coins at my feet,
I thanked them.

When they laughed to see me scramble in the mud,
I looked in their eyes and I laughed, too.

After the Idols

Maybe they can save each other's lives,
the old men gathered on the steps of the mosque
to smoke, read the tabloids or talk sports, whatever:

how all this was olive groves, even the sea gone
gray with abundance; what they did when they caught
that enemy pilot, knowing what losing would mean.

Now Nirvana blares from the cobbler's shop.
And not a week ago a boy sprang up in class
with a handgun, killing three children, why?

Maybe dusk, which glides in under the radar.
That a man can leave his job bone weary,
loosen his belt, prop his feet on the balcony

and watch the first star rise above his toes,
the chant, calling the faithful to prayer,
dying out in the brightly lit hills.

Crossing Iowa

Settled by the elect, the prairie's been saved from wandering the wilderness.
A few stands of trees circle the fields like oxen yoked to their stone mills.

The days are flat and brittle, and any change in the routine
is a lake you had better not walk across.

Beauty is emptiness: to drown.

It is emptiness to walk through the parking lot, the air so still and cold
your own breath floats before you like boats on an ink-black sea.

Even now, I could go back to Izmit and sleep in my bed again.

Off-Season

What isn't for sale is closed for the winter. The trawlers
slap against the wharf, huddled three deep, and the men
come by to drink and talk, fiddle with their nets awhile,
not one of them under forty. The masts creak in the wind,

and in the forest across the harbor the beech trees creak and break,
quicker than they grow new shoots, quicker than the dunes advance
from their protected enclaves, killing the roots, stripping the bark.
The outer rings dry up one by one, but the rot begins at the center.

On the beach the waves are soldiers from the First World War
running for the enemy's trenches, as if there is no death, only victory,
their soft bodies falling, the hard wind pushing them back.
The survivors retreat, join the others, and attack, regroup, and attack.

Just outside town, the sand-hazard sign flashes yellow.
Most drive on through, leaving their cars pocked with tiny craters.
Others take the detour. The dune grass bows and stands up,
bows and stands up. The Twenty-First Century belongs to Islam.

The Locust Moon

squats orange and pregnant on the horizon.

Every ending, said the Ancients, is really a beginning.

The air turned orange with their wings, unbreathable, almost.

When one night humid as this and drunk, a man scratched his name in
       the soil,

and stood there swaying and staring. The stick, the color of the clay.

       Thinking *think*.

II

Untitled Meridians

for Kerry

1

Half in the matter universe, and half outside, where things are ideas,
twilight begins in the water tower of the unincorporated town of
Progress. Contours deepen, and are lost. All is 2-D, a "living exhibit" in a
museum. The last defenders of objectivity write bitterly in discredited
journals. They have no power now that wanting a thing to be true makes
it so. Each cult believes in the end, which new meanings, who besides
themselves will emerge. When the Apocalypse comes we'll answer to
the unborn children, I voted yes, or I voted no, and on that we will
be judged.

2

A butterfly crosses the highway, having wandered away from the spice
trails only to find itself trapped in the Twentieth Century. In this world,
we still have highways. The airships never arrived from the home world,
making one sky under the blue flag. We have an inside and outside,
random wants. We don't have to kill each other for the Peace of a
Thousand Years. In this world I can say, my heart. Open it. Keep it shut.

Crossing Fort Pitt Bridge by Foot

Gray sky, white river. A chipmunk drinks from a water fountain. On
  the far bank,
leaves stir in the hold of a river barge, yellow paint rusting to orange.
A man drags a brick from a burnt-out warehouse and heaves it onto his
  pickup.
He has no sons to help him, or to ask what they think of *that*.
when the host of the all-talk gospel show tells a caller what to do about
  the in-laws' constant visits,
citing scripture: chapter, verse. Someone has written HELL AWAITS on a
  railing in the middle of the bridge.
FRANK AND ARMAND WORKING warns a girder nearby.
In the stadium to the right, a thousand men and women raise their hands
  high, and singing, jump,
and the leaves of the great elms flutter on their stems, each one distinct,
  and this is one game we haven't lost.
The light falls on a hillside, skips the one beside it, falls farther down,
  the clouds changing too,
so that the valley swings out of sight and opens again to the next one
  and the next and the one after that;
but how can it be beautiful to want sons this badly, and not be given
  any sons?

Sundays Are for Building Arks in the Afternoon

We've played this game all morning: you go to the front door, I open it,
you raise your tail and go to the back, as if the weather will be better there.
If it's just that you remember nothing, then all we know of hope is wrong.
You lay on the couch exhausted, a hairpin between your paws,
ears pointed forward in the fighting stance – poor sport after mole
        and rabbit,
I know. If that doesn't fill the loneliness time makes when we notice
        it's passing,
I'll kiss the fur above your nose, watch the rain with you if you like.

When I was your age, I would pass such days doing jigsaw puzzles.
The best was an ark I built over and over. As I held the elephant's trunk
        one day
grandfather wandered out in his slippers, bent to help. He had been
        a partisan
in the steppes of Anatolia, with just a canteen and a six-shooter to fight
        the Occupation –
and a rage that burned like embers in simple men across the country
until it became one fire. He became a mayor, wrote a novel.
He had no idea what the jagged square with the purple shape was for.

You flex your claws, moan. Perhaps you are dreaming of crows,
        your nemeses,
who chased you away from the porch so you ran back to me
ashamed. I should have stroked your tail lowered in defeat, told you
what a brave hunter you are. Later, I watched you bat a jay
across the lawn, let it escape, capture it, turn your back, patiently
wearing it down until it lay there refusing to escape, exhausted,
so it would not be so afraid. Little soul, when you die, is it forever?

Chronophobia

Light falls from our eyes and the honeybees start dying,
the leaves and the grass, then the soil freezes,
and children no longer play in the schoolyard, where it is unsafe.

Let the decrees set the clocks running backward
and the orbs rise in the grayness,
sweeping across the cornfields looking for warmth.

When the atoms spread out like pawns on a chessboard,
one on each square, a hundred billion years from now,
what is most vulnerable will still be hidden in plain sight.

I wish I were a cockroach crawling between the walls, the inside and
       the outside,
tasting the plaster and stale wood, touching their outlines, tasting them,
so mindlessly awake the city might be lying in ruins, no trace remaining
       of our wants.

I wish I were an airplane crossing the ocean by night.

Futility

I

The highway is going to hell in northern Wyoming.
What with the drought, the interstate bypass,
AFTER HIM UNDER THE SUN? — ECCELIAS
hanging from a withered billboard, the church house burnt.
As if it had meandered through the stunned grass for
       a thousand years,
and no longer believed we'll come back.

II

The man who staked this place
learned the difference between want and need.
That a strand of barbed wire could keep anything out
except what they call the elements, maybe,
and whoever took the trouble to trespass.
The elements that make a man.
Calcium. Sodium. Quartz. Part
compassion for the woman he called good.
When he'd speak of the fullness of time
as if it was a thistle he spat out —
that was want.

III

Believe me.
I would change the meaning of poor.
I wish I were a shard of stained glass
a boy exploring the ruins
picks up and turns over, saying glass.
I wish the bones of a small white bird
would rise up out of the prairie,
rise up and fly off in any direction.

IV

The Big Dipper hangs on its peg
over an empty rain barrel.

Trust

I

Even here,
among the cornstalks frozen in the mud,
so sharp they could impale the wind,
which flings its arms wide, and is gone.

II

Even here,
the woman who loves me still
keeps wanting to know
for what crime she was abandoned.

The Seal and the Seagull

I

Even now, survival is godhead, a dim red glow warming the water
      in the swollen lungs, resisting
each wave that tumbles it along the rocks, snapping the small bones,
      bursting the cells of protective blubber
made for the body's weight and roll, ice floes and the freezing wind,
      the crash of seal against seal.

II

He goes in through the eyes. The meat is rich and wholesome. Swings
      his beak like a pickax, strikes at the wounds, the flippers,
      anywhere,
paces the chest with his wings outstretched, barking in rage like a mad
      Ahab shaking his fist at the sea.

III

So this is what it's like. Coming by each day with your hands in your
      pockets to measure its progress,
a sandbar eroding there, a channel widening, the flipper torn off now,
      and secretly thrilled like a schoolboy
watching a dirigible crash and burn, all in slow motion, with zoom cuts
      and the purred narration.

IV

You could have brought some bread to share, brought a handful of smooth
      stones black from the sea.
You could have chosen pity, feeding the tide the broken bones to see what
      might come back

Man in God

The moon sometimes wanders past my backyard;
part light, part clay, part sleep, half insane
watching the white ash falling from the stars
make him a wife. They will try to ease the solitude
that wasn't my fault, and will fail each other
till I close the curtains, and trusting I'll rise
the next day, sleep, and sleeping, die.

A meteor streaks overhead,
its tail the arc of a classical tragedy.
As if I had tried to suspend it like a musical note,
dared stop the decay, had judged,
and failed you my prophet, oh, my prophet.

Glacier

I can imagine how it must have been, the glacier
so cold it wasn't snow that fell
but light,
the infrared cooling to ultraviolet,
breaking down
as it touched your coat and slid off
the visible spectrum,
I could have done so much
vanishing
word by word as you said it,
then the bearings: things, direction.

Meteorology

A storm front wanders down from the mountains, gray and white
      as Rip van Winkle, and as dazed, unable
to decide between rain and snow, and whose city this is, and what does
      YEAR NOW mean spray-painted on the walls.

If it rains, you'll watch the windshield wipers trudging right to left,
      a chained elephant lifting first one leg, then another,
and think of the days left till the weekend, and the weeks till a short
      vacation, and the year slipping away,

and being young blame only the sameness of things, how it would all be
      different, somewhere with somebody else,
the rain erasing their passage even before the wiper blades can complete
      a turn, the ads all saying, buy now, pay later.

Or the snow swirls between the buildings, solemn and frenzied as a ghost
      dance, and you look up at the rooftops vanishing,
to the commuters stamping their feet, their coats bunched at the collar,
      almost invisible, and the exhaust from cars,

and imagine it would be different some other time or place, the snow so
      thick it could almost be happening,
the other riders wrapped in themselves like explorers lost in a blizzard.
      Then they're gone, too, and you could be anything.

Ursa's Way

The night lurches past my trailer, an alcoholic dancing bear.
Past the guy next door beating up on his girl friend,
someone to make the pain go away like a torn blouse.
Past an old woman rocking in a rocking chair,
her children flown, her first husband killed in Dresden –
the cat rubs against her legs and purrs, the kettle boiling.
Past a storm front goose-stepping through New Orleans,
past a camp and across a bonfire, father and son lost
in their thoughts: in the light their faces flicker and change.
We have lived a hundred thousand lives;
I am tired of it all.
Carry me off on your rolling shoulders.
Show me a new way to live with myself.

Rune

It is the song of your tires on the pavement,
the car sliding over

the white dashes, then the arrowheads appearing
one-two-three

like targets in a shooting gallery
to show which way the road curves.

It is three stones etched with "opening:"
one for the inward and one for the future,

a pyramid tipped on its side.
You press "play," press "fast forward."

It is three frames from a movie.
It is the "less than" sign repeated three times.

Another Country

First rain of the rainy season:
you never get used to it,
the beautiful false dawn of the skyline
empty of you, Gastown empty –
the men on the waterfront throwing freight
exactly what they seem, and you,
facedown on your bed, unable to understand.
Never the mother-may-I, swaying on their stems,
nodding yes, yes you may.
You never get used to waking up to yourself.

Because rain strokes the face of the waters,
saying I am so lonely,
and the waters allow it, quiet in their depths,
saying lonely, owe me, yes.
Because the days walk down another street,
round the corner, and find
you again, maybe just a little changed.
Once upon a time there were carriages and horses.
There were ribbons in her hair.

Without Us

In the time it takes for a leaf to fall from a maple tree after a hard gust, we
were gone.

The moon was a light in the sky once more.

When the wolves came out of hiding, it was they who brought the little
ones down, and licked their paws clean afterward.

First the leader, then each according to its rank, their intelligent yellow
eyes aglow, watching for signs of weakness.

Red ants running on a bear's tongue. Fields of broccoli starting to bloom.

III

Magic

It is the oven burns
on the arms of a doll
she hugs and strokes

saying, Bad! Bad girl!
which translated means
I want to live.

It is a gray light rain
in a small industrial city,
somewhere in the mid-afternoon,

the mountains so much loose change
a waitress sweeps into her apron,
having made crew boss already.

It is a slick magician
who whisks off his black cape
to show us the empty cage,

and the rabbit's still there,
just sitting there
twitching its nose or something.

Work

The blue door has vanished now, dreamer. The dark shapes that kept
        you awake assume their proper forms and purpose.
Good Morning America starts the dull thumping down the hall that ends
        with her clothes strewn on the sidewalk,
the clothes small and quiet like the rain, the concrete sad and flat
        like the washed gray of worry in the predawn.

Outside, the traffic's begun, and the week ahead is so familiar it's almost
        a comfort now, a foghorn sounding its one note, then the sea
        flickering, fog, duration.
Like the faint, mechanical heartbeat of sleepers traveling between
        the stars. You're a swimmer turning for air every four strokes,
        waiting for wreckage, the shore to appear.
For the call in the predawn to snatch yourself back again, your old self
        vibrant before you, your mission clear, irrevocable,
as if the small voice were a man in a trench coat, and you, the awakened
        deep-cover agent from the episode called "The Sleeper."

Little princess tossing on a pea, the Cold War is over, and the nursery
        song about the bells remains the same in every language.
I would drink of you where your collarbone makes a cup, let the bus's
        low hydraulic hiss seal your double away.
I would share my sandwich with you and listen to jazz on the plaza
        of US Steel while the lunch crowd swirls around us
like a cheap electric clock: that is the only world we'll know if we should
        betray us: why it's useful to keep us so tired.

I wish we were two cats snug on a window ledge, watching the pigeons
        coo outside, comparing our figures, checking them twice.

Dedication

for Mau-Mau Kitty, whose name contains the mantra Aum,
the spoken essence of the Universe, a sacred blessing,
and the supremest affirmation

Who wiped out every pigeon on our roof save two, so that the plenty
would be replenished, thus advancing agriculture;
who patiently licked the mouse he brought us so its fur flowed without
ruffles, a study of curves and texture;
who hugged the black cat Tar to his chest as they fell arm in arm from
the balcony into the bushes two flights below, and touched noses
after, thus proving the theorem Peace through Strength;
whose ears are shaped like the arches of the Taj Mahal, whose pupils
open like the dome of a telescope, who purrs in the musical
patterns of the Spheres;
who takes such pleasure in the simple joys – draping his tail over his eyes
to sleep, drinking water from a running tap – you can truly
believe we'll be raised incorruptible, too, someday;
whose paws have fur between them, for he loves the season when snow
melts and the trees burn their green candles;
who can round corners at a gallop and jump ten times his height at will,
for his whiskers are half the length of his tail;
whose white paws are wisdom and black paws are gentleness, who can
shift his shape at night, who can walk through walls.

Three Rivers

What are you doing, Anne-Marie, on the night we would bring home
    good things to cook and watch movies from the 1940s, the work
    week finally ended?

Who will light the stove for you now that I'm not there?

I imagine you in our city of bridges, where the Midwest flows into the
    East and South, singing.

What with the apple trees baring their branches, the light "like no other
    that I've seen before, Alpay, worn and soft,"

and your new coat that matches the color of your hair perfectly, so that
    you cross the lawn to the Cathedral of Learning trailing
    footprints in the frost;

what with Mau-Mau Kitty, who leaves presents in our bed for you, their
    fur licked in one direction and their heads neatly reattached, so
    they will be pleasing to the eye as well,

do you still look for me, for a moment, when you swing into our favorite
    cafe, in our neighborhood named for its squirrels?

When I come home at last in the season of cherry blossoms in the rain,
    will you still love me?

You've started saving magazines again, bus passes, too, and receipts from
    the grocery store. Colored paper clips. Our apartment's
    crammed with old sea shells, from the winter we lived on
    the Cape.

When Mr. Lobster visits my Jacuzzi, no one tries to talk me into setting
him free in the harbor: the days are long and silent:

I drop him in, and we watch each other through the steam.

I'm driving home from the airport without you. I feel sad in my stomach.

One Good Reason

I had been traveling all day through the fall colors, hugging the
      mountainside
in long, majestic thunder-glides of sweep and easy speed, as if I'd already
      been here

but had never felt anything like it. The Earth's enormous curve and spin
      and the car
perfectly aligned, the leaves I'd gathered to bring you scattered beside me
      for good luck.

Then the road descending. Rain. Local traffic and its routines. Clouds
      piled up
like dishes in the sink. Then the sign, BLUE MOUNTAIN, 500 FEET.

It's been twelve hundred years, and the moon is still not interested
      in drinking.
I lower the wine, embarrassed, and have a swig for both of us.

Li Po watched the moon cross over to the other side of the Milky Way
and said to himself the moon I'll meet you there,

Immaculate Radiance of Being, Mind of My Mind, Beautiful
Friend. Thinking: Li Po danced with his shadow, he was so lonely.

If I ran into you twenty years late, at the Blue Mountain Restaurant
      and Bar,
would we recognize each other anymore?

What is happiness if it's built on chance?
Li Po, what is enlightenment?

In another world I'm climbing Blue Mountain, drunk, with my begging
       bowl full
and the Zen ocean whooshing around my head, humming
       a snatch of blues.

Willow

It is a woman washing clothes by the riverbank.
It is the end of a frayed rope.
It is the weave of the water vendor's chant in the air
in my neighborhood in Istanbul, with its narrow maze of streets.
It is a mortal that the gods had pitied,
so that her soul was visible, but we could no longer hurt her.
She had beautiful pianist's fingers.
It is the nerves that send the eyes' charged impossible messages back.

What are you now, Po Chü-i?
It is a map of the freeways of the City of Angels,
the legs of two enormous insects copulating.
Are you still afraid of the Yangtze River, or have you become a white ox
            drinking from it?
It is the work of a boy drawing squigglies with his crayons,
one in purple, one in pink, as a present to his father.

Three Wishes

Would we become immortal?
Would we walk naked through the forests
which had been waiting all these centuries for our return?
Would we grow wings?
What would we do?
What would we do with our past?
Would we make it up to everyone we wronged,
use those second chances we'd been letting slide?
What would we know if we knew the future?
Would we speak the languages of streams?
Would we bring the dodo back? The cockatrice? The magestic
       pterodactyls?
What would we say to the Swiss Alps?
Would we still carve sandstone into great cathedrals?
Would we still burn witches?
Would we still have revolutions?
Would we walk around all night to avoid our apartments, my friend?
What would we do about the smog?
What would we do with the Antarctic?
Would we make it bloom?
Would we have perpetual twilight?
I love twilight.
I should like a shot of whiskey, please.
I love winter mornings,
snow falling out of the clear blue.

Homage

(James Wright, Po Chü-i)

Last night I dreamt I was a Chinese Wild Man
who cut off his white beard under the wandering lights of heaven

and flung it at them,
having served the Emperor as soldier, husband, father, clerk,

and now this.
I had been reading the *Rand McNally* road maps of America,

tracing the back roads with my finger,
thinking of home.

The surf rises on the beach like the steps of an escalator
as if this were a country where no one had to die in vain,

yet all your thinking got you was a mouthful of black earth,
the spirit ponies you rode through the pueblos gone forever,

only Ohio still real.
It must be very beautiful, therefore, where you are,

at the other end of that frayed rope
you thought you'd hold a thousand years,

wanting either to be rid of it and wander away disgraced
or be pulled up the Yangtze River to the village for exiles on the frontier,

never to return. Are you still lonely?
Or have you forgotten your old name, even in passing?

Knowing the Emperor's cruel hoax finished not only your career,
how did it come to you to break into blossoms instead?

Planting a Garden

I

All day the birds have been twittering advice from their perches,
the fat one an expert in snow peas, the other a strawberry connoisseur,
strutting around the periphery and flying off again to interview
      each other
live on location, even the ones from competing trees, finally even
      the squirrels.
My job is to carry things, and sit on the porch and smoke.
The cat is helping, too. He is lying in the sun with his paws before him
like some Egyptian god, his thoughts warm and fluid, geometric, alert,
      watching
you tear the grass by its roots, your fingers deep in earth so lush
"Jack and the Beanstalk" must have been set here.
If "dark and rich" were a color, what a strange thing having a body
      would be.
No one would ever be afraid of death again.
If "dark and rich" were a color, "Anne-Marie" would look up from
      the garden
and two hundred years slip away like a glass of water tipped on its side.

II

No shadows. Only the heat and its odorless, translucent flowers, and the
      villa's stark white walls.
Tomato plants, hard and distinct, laid out in little rows like artifacts from
      an ancient city, their names written neatly below.
As if they would crumble like a clod of earth if you grasped one to snap
      off a sucker, your fingers crumbling too, then your palm, the
      back of your hand.
You part your lips and the heat sears your lungs: you don't remember if
      you spoke, or just thought the words.
You don't remember what you thought: the heat, your lips.

Someplace green perhaps, like the meadow you strolled hand in hand
    with your father when you were just a girl, barely able to walk,
    how you're older than he was that day.
What a strange thing to have a body. You suppose you should put some
    water in it.
You should stand up now with your shirt clinging to your breasts and your
    face to the small breeze any movement would make.
For a long time you consider the sky, rooted there like a white flower,
    motionless, waiting for rain.

III

A dry leaf tumbles into a puddle and sways at the water's edge, a galleon
    loading provisions, waiting for dusk, for the Ancient World
    to return.
Like a mother watching that strange light go out in her newborn's eyes so
    she can rest, knowing he's here now.
Ivy twists around and around the daylilies like wolves corralling a herd
    of wild horses.
They raise their necks in terror and the wolves jump, pulling them down.
The ants swarm from a corner of the garden, blind in their armor, to
    carry the empire off in fragments for the red queen's pleasure.
A beetle disappears into the same darkness it has always known: the cat
    slits its eyes and swallows, not from hunger, not for anything.
In the center: tools: what is and what will be marked by stakes and a
    piece of string: an ashtray flooded with rainwater, mosquitoes
    breeding in it.
When it seems you've forgotten that you asked I tell you, for your Anne-
    Marie–ness, irreducible, for the wake the wind cuts in the grass.

Lullaby

You are safe.
You are lying in a hammock
far from the cult of the black sun,
the folded wings of the sky over Portland.
Far from the mantra *information*.
You don't have to justify your life.
You could be a flower,
your own thoughts falling around you like rain.
You could be the timber wolf
who has lain in ambush a hundred thousand years
for the flying horse to land once more.
Sleep steps lightly over the wet grass, cocks its head.
The highway ribbons through the mountains
and vanishes into the afternoon.
The light is pale and clear.
It feels good to listen to the thunder.

West

New shoots out of the logging road,
cool gauze of cumulus to soothe the deep river gorge,
even the picnic tables warped by rain and eaten by termites
to heal the part we cut away: to smell wood smoke is ambrosia.
It is ambrosia to listen to the small voice speak again.

In the north, thunder heralds heavy rain.
A crow lifts itself up sullenly and slogs toward shelter:
the play of grays and greens: to think and to feel.
A chipmunk grasps its acorn like a little treasure: he is so happy
his cheeks are bursting: the air is thick with good scents to smell

and there is time to smell them all
and room for lightning and for leaves to turn in the rain,
for the oldest trees to fall, and the others, stunted in shadow, to emerge.
There's room for the picnic lodge and the mushrooms under the doorstep.
It is ambrosia to breathe and to grow.

A car drives by, headlights on. The crunch of wheels on gravel
and the heater's low warm din lull the children asleep in the backseat.
A coyote crosses over to the other side, his eyes bright with hunger.
There's time for smoke to rise from the cooking fire.
It is ambrosia to look and to see.

Acknowledgments

Thanks to the editors and publishers of the following journals, where these poems appeared, some in revised versions:

Black Warrior Review:	"Willow"
Gettysburg Review:	"July" "One Good Reason" "Three Rivers" "Chronophobia" (originally as "Fall")
Hayden's Ferry Review:	"Homage"
The Literary Review:	"Dedication"
Malahat Review:	"Bad Thoughts, Mixed Messages" "Planting a Garden"
Northwest Review:	"Ars Poetica"
Poor Tom:	"History" "Trust" (originally as "East")
Prism:	"After the Idols" "Glacier" "Heat Lightning, Progress, Cat, George Orwell" "Man in God"
Witness:	"Crossing Fort Pitt Bridge by Foot" "The Seal and the Seagull"

Some of these poems were broadcast on National Public Radio's *Iowa Radio Project*, and on WOMR's *Works in Progress*.

Thanks to these organizations for their generous gifts of time and money: Bucknell Seminar for Younger Poets, Fine Arts Work Center in Provincetown, Helene Wurlitzer Foundation in New Mexico, Iowa Arts Council, and the Edna St. Vincent Millay Colony.

About the Author

Alpay Ulku was born in Turkey, grew up in Canada, finished high school in England, and has lived throughout the United States. He received a BA from the University of Redlands (Johnston Center) and an MFA from the Iowa Writers' Workshop, and was a second-year fellow at the Fine Arts Work Center in Provincetown, Massachusetts. His work has appeared in many literary magazines, including *Black Warrior Review, Gettysburg Review, Malahat Review,* and *Witness.* Alpay lives in Pittsburgh with his wife, the writer Anne-Marie Gallagher, and their Maine Coon cat, Mau-Mau Kitty Gallagher-Ulku, and writes operations manuals for a living.

BOA EDITIONS, LTD.:
The A. Poulin, Jr. New Poets of America Series

Printed in the USA
CPSIA information can be obtained
at www.ICGtesting.com
JSHW082226140824
68134JS00015B/746